Free Will
Vibes of Rhythm Divine

POLYGLOT/AUTHOR
KUNWAR BAHADUR SINGH

INDIA · SINGAPORE · MALAYSIA

ISBN
Paperback 979-8-89744-261-4
Hardcase 979-8-89984-222-1

God Ganesa also known as Ganpati, Vighnaharta, Lambodara and Vinayaka is son of God Shiva and Goddess Maa Parvati. Ganesa is the God of prosperity, good luck and success. Before any auspicious work to start Hindus first worship Lord Ganesa.

In Sanskrit God Ganesa means God of the Ganas. Gana means councils or assemblies convened to discuss matters of religion or other topics. In Hinduism, the Ganas are attendants of Shiva and live on Mount Kailash. Ganesha was chosen as their leader by Shiva, hence Ganesa's title gaṇeśa or gaṇapati, "God or leader of the ganas".

Therefore, instead of appeasing each Gana in order to receive their respective blessings, we bow to their God, Sri Ganesha. By receiving his grace, we receive the grace of all. God Ganesh removes any potential obstacles and enables us in our endeavours and supports us to succeed.

*Dedicated in the service
of humanity with hopes*

Disclaimer, or use at your own wisdom

This disclaimer informs readers that the views, thoughts, and opinions expressed in the texts, poems belong to the original author(s) and not that of compiler, author himself, author alone, author's employer, organization, committee, or another group or individual that the author is or was associated.

Much of the inspiration that is expressed through texts, poems, is influenced from various sources and most of which are many decades old and should be put into practice with caution. The way of life described may not be apt in the current or future ages.

The author does not make any warranties about the completeness, reliability, and accuracy of this information. Any action taken upon the information is strictly at readers own wisdom and the author will not be liable for any loss or damages in connection with the use of the information provided.

Special thanks to Deepak Bose, Amit Arora & Digant Singh for converting my personal poems into a shape of a book

What's the fight, settle it,

Why do you keep fighting with yourself?

You are very much dangerous,

Don't you know yourself?

Every happiness is for you, so be happy in sorrowful days.

Leave the tears for me,

Because I am here to bear all your pains.

The God makes use of broken things, very
beautifully.

When the clouds break, it rains continuously,

The soil takes a form of fertile field when it is
broken.

The seed takes a form of young plant when it
is broken.

So, if you feel broken then consider it as God's
grace,

As God wants to use you for any good
purpose.

It's time for the sun to rise,

It's time for the flowers to blossom,

Wake up from the sweet sleep O' my friend,

It's time to fulfil the dream.

When they are alive,

They never follow their advice.

They will also never ask,

About the condition of their health.

But when they passed away from this world,

Then they search their lost will to get the wealth.

Memories drive us mad, and the things drive
us crazy,

The day passes, but the night drives us crazy.

When two things are together one is wealth,
and the other is health,

Then old age passes very comfortably.

I have a habit of mixing with everyone,
I love a habit of creating my own identity.
No matter, how deep wound someone has
given to me,
I have a habit of smiling equally and sweetly.

Why I am the only one who thinks?

That he might be feeling bad.

Why does not anyone else think?

That I might be also feeling bad.

She must have lost something like me,

I have lost my desire she lost her loved one.

She was a story and it kept changing,

I was a book and remained like a book without any change.

Meeting was coincidence, and separation was destined,

She went as far away as she was close to me.

It is our habit to smile all the time,

Our wish is that you remain happy like this all
the time.

Did you remember us or not,

But it is our habit to remember you all the
time.

She used to bow her head in shame,

She used to smile in grace.

As long as the lover's heart knows,

How to handle it.

She used to throw down the thunder bolt.

True love is that which neither increases nor decreases,

And remains the same in every situation.

Such love is for the whole world,

and it is also equal for the whole world in every condition.

The is the truest form of love for all,

And this kind of love is the form of almighty.

The one who has love always in his heart for everyone,

His life is only happy.

I do not know why that man is angry
with me.

The man talks about me but does not
talk to me.

Last year, I was afraid of losing you,

This year, I am afraid of that I may not
encounter you.

Every breath seems to me as last breath,

Neither we are dying, nor we are living.

He understands that every person changes,

He thinks that the whole world is like his
understanding.

The meaning of the love was the name of a
boy for her,

But it was not acceptable to anyone,

So, the boy left the girl and went away.

In spite of all this,

The heart of the girl could not go away from
the heart of the boy.

O' little bird, O' little bird,

You are very little.

Your diet is also not more,

So, eat also little.

Do not eat one complete maize.

Otherwise, when you will drink water, then
you will die.

So, eat less, and live alive.

O' little bird, O' little bird.

People like us are like glass,

Sometimes we break, sometimes we are broken
by others.

Everyone knows his deeds.

That's why there is so much crowd on the
bank of river Ganges.

Crying to get her, getting her, and losing her
again,

If this is the love, then we are better off alone
in this world.

There is lot to say in the heart of that man,

The man who remains very silent in this
world.

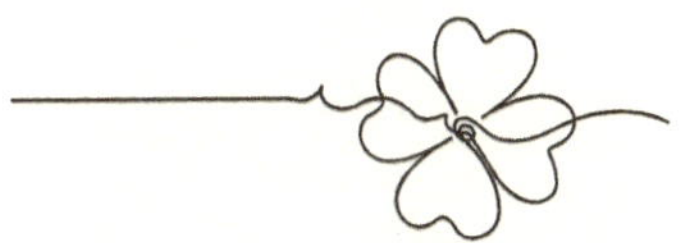

You must forget that what hurt you,

But do not forget that what it taught to you.

People say that it hurts,

When someone close to you goes away,

But it hurts more,

When someone goes away despite being close
to you.

The ability to give happiness to everyone is not
in your hands.

But the ability to not hurt anyone is in your
hands.

The beauty of the life does not depend on that
how happy you are?

Rather, it is about that how many people are
happy with your deeds.

The days organised a crowd and formed a year.

Who says that time does not die,

We have seen the year end in the month of
December,

Sometimes ago,

I left you while writing my diary.

Even today,

I remember you when I turn the pages of my
diary.

She said softly after hugging me in the
gathering,

This is the tradition of the world.

Do not consider it as my love.

You smile at condition,

It's my curse that you too fall in love with
someone.

I love only your soul,

Although there may be so many lovers of your
face.

Your love made me devotee of God.

Although I have heard that people become
drunkards after falling in love.

I will spend my whole life waiting for you,

If you promise to come back again in my life.

A flower falls from the branch of the time.

One year passed like every time.

Some dreams could not turn into reality,

Some dreams were turned into reality.

Some faces were liked, and some were not in
my heart.

The fabric of the time will be rebuilt.

Some new stories will be made again from
tomorrow.

Some stories will be repeated from tomorrow.

Let us welcome the coming of the new year.

The earth thrilled,

The sky smiled,

There is a feeling, an emotion, and a
loveliness.

A hope, a trust and a newness.

A desire, a dream, and a hypothesis.

This is the beginning of the new year.

Let us welcome the coming of the new year.

If you follow the advice that you give to others,

You will succeed in your life.

Look for that feedback that challenges you,

Do not look for the validation from the one
that gives you peace.

If you remember me in your free time,

Then let it be.

This world is for the pretty face.

The pure hearted are left here.

We may be alone,

But we are not useless.

Every journey has an end,

Be it life or lies.

The pain also has its own style,

It loves those who tolerate it.

Only small happiness becomes the
support of life,

What about desires those keep changing
every moment.

A person whose mind is calm,

Everybody feels peace around him, even his opponents also praise him.

This rule applies to every creature and to the nature.

People of the evil nature also give up, evils in the company such people.

The law of deeds works here.

The law of deeds is of great use.

The storms died after banging their heads,

With the desire to destroy the trees.

The trees saved themselves,

Those had the skill of bending.

The world is very much cruel, people will
consider you dead,

And bury you in the grave,

So even if you sleep,

Keeping your legs moving.

Kunwar Bahadur Singh § 33

We have tested all types of love,

But if love is one sided then the fun is
something else.

Now I am just looking for Him,

After meeting whom, there is no need of
anyone.

The true form of happiness, and sorrow is the
like lake within us.

Sometimes the waves of the humour rise in it
which is filled without tears.

The deeper the lines that grief will
draw in our souls,

We will be able to fill it with that much joy.

The reason for the happiness is the same which
was sadness yesterday.

Do not fight with the Sun so much,

The night tells us every day.

Protect me from the evil eyes,

Do not show me the mirror in this way.

Do not be so sad,

That you did not reach to your destination.

There are still many people here,

Who do not even know the way.

When a man gets success in love,

He gets amazing success,

but if he fails, he scatters badly.

People considered me gold in the market,

But you did not consider me even equal to clay,

One gets respect those who respect others.

This is not my complaint,
but this is my experience.

She asks me a question every day,

If I had fallen in love with her,

But the lives were not placed at stake.

Many people do every work unwillingly.

They use only some part of their concentration purposely.

Therefore, they do not have power to get to the destination.

Whereas the secret of the success lies in concentration.

When there is a new year in life.

There is a new pleasure in life.

There is a new excitement in life.

There is a new policy in life.

Then this is the victory of life.

Peahen dance, peahen dance with delight.

The clouds are covering the sky in rainy season.

Why should you not remember your loved one in such situation.

Peahen dance in every courtyard with merriment.

Peahen dance, peahen dance with delight.

There is greenery all over the earth with loveliness.

The branches of the trees are decorated with buds and flowers.

Peahen dance in honey garden with enjoyment.

Peahen dance, peahen-dance with delight.

The wind is full of lovely fragrances.

Peahen dance, peahen dance with delight.

We have written story of your love on our
heart.

Neither a little nor a lot but I have written it
beyond limit.

So, include us also in your prayers some time.

We have written our every breath in your
name.

Whoever wants to grow the crop, may grow
the crop.

But you keep flowing like a stream of water
everywhere.

Do not stop the velocity of your inner
sentiments due to any misgiving.

You keep singing the feelings arising in your
heart by making a song.

Man sacrifices his health to earn money.

Then he spends money to stay healthy.

Man is so shaken about the future that he cannot enjoy the present.

The result of all this is that neither he lives peacefully in the future nor in present.

Man lives as if he is never going to die.

Thus, the man dies without enjoying a real life.

You are the throat of life, so do not break its
courage.

You should not stop the impulse of your life,
and express your grief with care.

You should let your heart roar, whatever the
voice, it wants to chide.

Do not worry about anyone, whose heart hurts
and where.

We are not immortal here; we have only been here for about few hundred years.

We should do something good in our life during these years.

We should do something useful and show generosity towards others.

We will find the meaning of life when we contribute to the happiness of others.

If the clouds of the emotions arise in your
mind, then do not stop them.

If the clouds of the emotion's rains nectar, then
do not stop them.

Do not run towards every vibration of life at all
the time.

You do not know that sometimes, the song
dies if it is not written on the time.

Sit deep inside your mind and listen to the
silent tinkling's of the mind.

Look in the light at the stars scattered across
the sky of the mind.

Sometimes by great fortune they blossom in
the sky of consciousness.

So, do not let your thoughts scatter on the
streets like this.

The best way to make own destiny beautiful is
to seek challenges with heart.

One must not only accept one's destiny.

But one must also love It with heart.

Only if you find a way out of beaten path,

then you will find something special.

The key to happiness probably lies in dealing
with the sufferings well.

Who will know the secret of what you are
trying to say?

O' Brother who will take you here through
your eyes?

You will appear as you are in their eyes.

Who will believe that you are a different light
from all these Human beings?

The fairy who has come into my life wearing a
magic shawl,

Is my name and fame worth nothing compared
to her beauty?

Will you not be able to digest the taste of this
secret in your mind?

Then you are truly still an imperfect lover of
the real beauty?

If there is humanity in the heart,

Then there will be beauty in the character.

When there is beauty in the character,

Then there will be harmony at the home and
in the behaviour.

If there is harmony at the home,

Then there will be order in the nation.

When there is order in the nation,

Then there will be peace in the world, and in
the world federation.

If a man asks question, then he becomes fool
for a while.

The man who does not ask questions remains
fool for his entire life.

Therefore, if you commit any mistake then do
not let it become a crime by feeling ashamed of
the end.

If you commit any mistake then, better to
commit it immediately, instead of feeling
embarrassed.

You went far away from yourself, leaving the
centre behind,

O' Traveller now is the time to go and find
yourself by leaving the path for a few days.

You yourself should light such a fire so that
you could possess a form of light on its own,

And do not let the pain remain in your heart
to increase the heat of the songs.

He who once makes a promise never backs out
is a brave.

A hermit is a one who drinks the pleasure but
does not say anything about its taste.

Well, everybody gets the flowers, but only few
get the fruits.

Those who do not reveal the secret of the tree
that grows in their hearts.

We do not know the way, where should we
go, and see you?

Some where your flute plays, this is all the
knowledge about you.

My smallness does not let me go above the top
of hill,

and hey God let my ego allow me to bow my
head to the soil.

You need good friends to be successful in your life.

You need enemies to be extremely successful in your life.

If you want victory in every game then, you will have to become an expert.

Life is just like a thin thread, and it takes a moment to break it.

If you want to find yourself.

Then do not look in the mirror, because there only a shadow of stranger peek inside yourself,

And so then if you will look at the whole world, everything will appear beautiful forever.

I touched the edge of the perimeter and return
again and again.

My desire to find you, and bring you back
remains unfulfilled again and again.

O' God how do you feel when I disturb you
again, and again with the fragrance of the
flowers.

Since when I troubled you by singing it, and
calling you on the path of truth,

so sometimes you say something to hide
yourself among the thicket of the leaves.

What should I ask a fire fly what pleasure do
you get in shining again and again and then
hiding?

What passion does a burning moth have, after
I keep wondering?

I believed that there is happiness in freedom,
but tell me then how do you feel after getting
caught in the net of a flower?

What is the pleasure of being trapped and
suffering in the net of a flower?

Just as the sunlight dispels darkness,

Similarly create that light within yourself
which can remove the darkness of your life.

There is a mystery behind your every step that
you take,

And which makes you forward in your life.

How can anyone be happy amidst so many
problems?

There is only one answer to this that we must
love everyone in our life.

We have seen that pretence destroys love,

So, you love everyone with the best mind in
your life.

I did not see your first photo.

That's why I did not recognize your last scene
properly.

I have heard the story of life has the beginning
and end only.

Since I did not know the destination, and I did
not even know the way.

It was certain that I would go, so I had gone
quietly.

I had not seen this world,

So, I had to walk a lot here.

I could not even stay in this valley,

because I had no business here.

Someday I will cross this world,

And jump into the ocean of salvation.

But there is no rest as the journey remains,

And there is also no salvation.

O' Dark night O' Dark night, O' Dark night

Give us sun rays and light.

The dark night has been haunting the human
like children for many ages.

O' God If the light's treasury empty then just
do this,

Set this world on fire,

So that there could be some light in this
darkness.

We are all artist,

And we can freely draw pictures according to
our imagination.

We must learn to imagine,

And the world should be made beautiful based
on imagination.

Logic and knowledge take us forward to
a certain extent, but imagination takes us
everywhere.

Imagination is more important, than logic and
knowledge in every sphere of human life.

Alas, the sorrow of my heart became a matter
of joy for you.

The stream of my tears from my eyes became
nectar of flowers for you.

You call me a poet, but how can this sad mind
of mine believe?

All I remember is that the sorrow in my heart
come out and become a poetry for everyone.

The company of honest people is very
important in our life.

The honesty is very expensive gift,

so do not expect this from cheap people.

The importance of honesty cannot be
underestimated and denied by anyone.

Just as the honesty of others is important.

Similarly, this is also important to be honest
with everyone.

Loveliness, loveliness, O' loveliness,

I have heard that the world is cup of honey
wine.

Here we get nectar on the lips,

And the eyes turn red due to wine.

Here youth always float on the waves of the
stream of love.

Here the drunken beautiful woman,

Always keep showering honey wine in the
man's life.

Hey bud, I love you more than even a bumble
bee loves you.

Hey cross on the riverbank,

You are sweeter than even the lips of my
beloved, so that I can kiss you.

Your sprouts you are also sweet,

And in the full moon light you are intoxicating
like a drunken queen.

But I am very sad that I am not immortal in
this pleasure garden.

The dawn will come laughing into this valley
filled with the greenery.

The bud will smile for ages, and cuckoo will
sing for many ages into this Valley.

There will be shower of joy on the earth by
mingling with the rays of the moon.

Only I will not be there,

but this sweet stream will keep on flowing into
this valley of mountain.

Loving humility is a wonderful weapon to win everyone.

You can buy the world with the priceless treasures of love.

The respect is linked with the love and that's why you must respect everyone.

Try to be sun so that everyone can look at you with hope.

If you want to get respect from others, then learn to respect yourself.

If you want to convert the world then first convert yourself.

The day when the sweet sound of

Your anklets were heard in the dense, desolate
wilderness.

That very day the life startled,

And all arteries of my heart became restless.

O' Goddess, you had imprisoned me in your
heart,

But I have found the paradise.

Although I am locked in your embrace,

But all the chains of the world have gone
loose.

O' beautiful lady my crazy imagination is
searching for you like a butterfly in the forest.

My soothing poem colours a picture of you
after sitting on the path of a desert.

I am poor, and after spreading my dreams on
the path of forest,

I am waiting for the drowsy bud to come.

I am sitting in my hut and waiting for the
queen of heaven to come.

Tomorrow the life will become death, and
death will become new life.

Then why is there rise, and fall between the
death, and life?

If the paint of life is immortal,

then what difference does it make whether I
become dust or a flower?

If life gives a smile, then why do you call
death are tears?

Hey darling wake up,

The night itself has brought a red crown for
you.

There is a new beauty across the water, sky, air,
stars, and trees for you.

The bumble bees have found the buds,

And the sun rays have found the water.

The night of the jealousy is now over, and
beloved has found his lover.

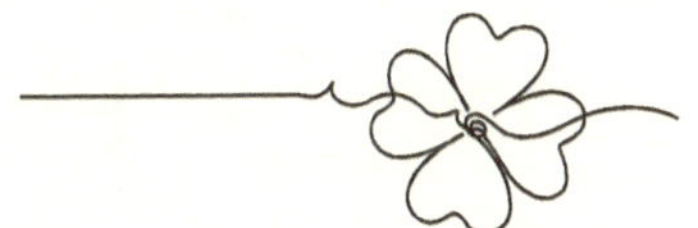

I am a faraway traveller,

And I want to stay here for a moment.

I am very tired, and I want to sit with beauty
for some time to entertain my intellect.

How do I resist the urge to take another sip of
liquor?

I want to go to a faraway country, but where
else will I get this pleasure?

Keeping anger in yourself means,

That you are holding fire in your hand to
throw it to someone else.

If you will keep love with in you then you will
be happy,

And other people will also feel pleasure.

Make yourself so strong that no kind of praise
or criticism,

Can make you feel a gentleman or a culprit.

A life for a few days and then nothing after all
the life ends.

You are born, you grow up and you are happy,
you want and then the life ends.

After all it is the moments of love,

That give meaning to the meaningless life.

Only if you will live in the present moment,

then you will be able to understand the love.

The more knowledge a man has, the closer he
is to good qualities.

When we live a simple and reasonable life
then we can get all the happiness.

Learning from everything, and everywhere
should be a part of man's life.

The continuous process of learning is the first
condition of a good life.

Every man can enjoy the good life and can
stand the test of his own qualities.

An active life is to reach the goals, and an idle
life deviates from the goals.

Kunwar Bahadur Singh § 77

If we look carefully then we will realise that life is a goal.

The life becomes dull, and burden without a goal.

Setting goal is what motivates us to struggle continuously in life.

The life is meaningful only when there is a goal in life.

The man who lives in harmony with nature
remains safe in the world.

There is no kind of attack on such kind of man
in this world.

He gets involved in his devotion and achieves
his motive.

The man who is happy, the reason for this is
that he does not have any arrogance.

The biggest obstacle to a person's success is his
arrogance.

A person must give up his ego to be successful
in human life.

The time has great importance in the man's life.

The one who recognized the value of time achieved a lot in life.

Many people fail, because they do not value time.

You will achieve everything in your life, if you will know the value of time.

O' brave man perform your duties with
bravery and increase your honour.

You should respond to your enemy with the
power of your will power.

They are not the brave man who torment
others.

True heroes are those who enhance the dignity
of others.

Even if it was coincidence but everyone has changed colours,

Everyone has shown their true face in front of everyone.

These people who were watching the spectacle of my drowning,

now they have set out with a boat to look for me.

I do not know how many dreams committed suicide,

By hanging on to the ropes of reality.

I had to fulfil my promise to life in this manner.

I wanted to cry openly but had to laugh loudly.

Learning a lesson is no small matter,

How can I say that I got nothing in return.

You should live every moment of life to the
fullest,

Because later there will be only memories,

And the time will not come back again.

When I look at someone then my eyes blink,

Only once because this is love.

It does not happen again and again.

The city of love is very crowded Sir!!

Whoever is lost here once never found again.

Kunwar Bahadur Singh § 85

Wounds heal with time,

But the noise of accident remains throughout
the life.

I have learned to say high fever now has
emitted heat,

I have learnt to smile like a stranger in my
own house.

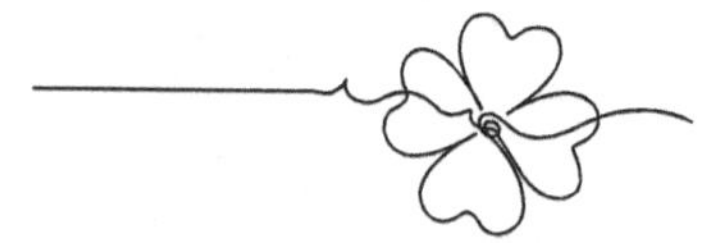

I like to talk to everyone,

but I have learnt not to say everything in front
of everyone.

You will find many more beautiful faces than
me,

but you will not find a heart like mine
anywhere.

I wanted to sell my tears in the market,

But every purchaser said that is a gift given,

By loved ones and cannot be sold to others.

I then stopped talking about it,

Because I did not want to share her with others.

Try being angry for a while,

Who will come to pacify you?

This will be enough if you want to test your
love.

A huge crowd gathered due to my shouting,

but the person I called did not come.

The time told me the truth about everyone,

Otherwise, I considered everyone as my well-wisher.

I was very much surprised after my death today,

Those who had kicked me were giving me shoulders.

The one who has experienced the magic of
prayer,

Can survive without food for many days.

But not for even a moment can survive
without prayer.

One should pray to awaken love for God in
one's mind,

Because there is no inner peace without prayer.

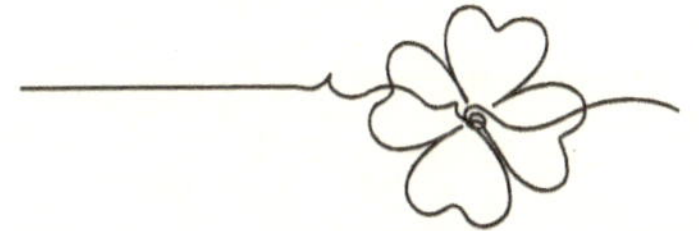

Neither it gets connected by staying close,

Nor it breaks by staying away.

Relationship is that thread of feelings,

Which gets stronger by remembering only.

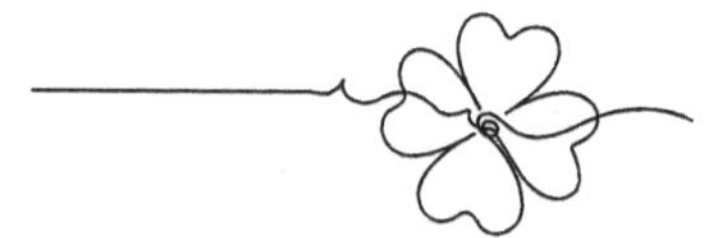

Falling in love with someone is not love sir,

The thing without which the heart cannot feel happy is called love.

Those people in whose life crying are written,

They fall in love with someone once in their life.

Sir doing injustice is not an easy game.

The heart must be made heartless, and
emotions must be eliminated.

The weak man must be found.

The weight of the benefit must be placed
heavily on the scale.

The compulsion of the compulsive must be
weighed with scheme.

One must avert eyes from the heart writhing
with pain.

It takes a lot of effort to prove an honest man
as dishonest,

And a truthful person as a false man.

Sir, doing injustice is not an easy game.

The story of my life is different.

Someone should learn from me to smile at every moment.

Everyone, please do not cast an evil eye on my smile.

I have endured a lot of pain then I have learnt to smile.

We have not changed at all,

But we have started understanding the world.

Companionship received for free is useless,

Solitude achieved through hard work is good.

I have spent a lifetime without you,

and now without you I may even die.

Love is as soft as wax,

but the same love made me stone.

Dreaming is a deception, and wakefulness is also a deception.

The past is just bragging, and future is just imagination.

The present is just like a surrender and future an illusion.

Dreaming is a deception and wakefulness is also Deception.

Man has no right here and we are so helpless,

That neither we can select anything, nor we can abandon.

Dreaming is a Deception, and wakefulness is also a deception.

I do not know who holds my neck and forces me,

To say that both life and death here has no significance.

Dreaming is a deception, and wakefulness is also a deception.

Where will I go if I will go away from you?

Where will I find a friend like you?

Anyhow, I will console my conscience.

But where will I hide my sorrowful face?

Come on my mind,

And go somewhere faraway, where there is no noise.

Our own welfare lies in the welfare of the
others.

Our own liberation and devotion,

Remain in the liberation and devotion of
others.

Our main duty should be the welfare of all the
creatures.

We should not have more desires,

but our objective should be welfare of others.

The whole world is like a beautiful flower,

And every country is like one of its petals.

This beautiful earth is more blessing from God,

Which the God has given to all living beings.

May its beauty never diminish and always be
alive and safe.

May it spread happiness, and fragrance to
everyone.

These are the two very difficult tasks in the
world.

First if you will tell the truth then you cannot
live in the world,

and second if you lie you cannot reside in
heaven.

Whose glory does not diminish by going to
someone else house?

The glory of the river Ganges ends as soon as
it meets the sea.

How can a weak man overcome a powerful
man by enmity with him?

How can one be in enmity with a crocodile
while living in the sea?

Who once sacrificed his life for me,

He used to accept whatever I said.

Who would recognize me from a distance.

Today, he passed by me unnoticed,

Let the storms of reality glow.

Who knows in what lust the mask might
blow.

Both birds look alike until they do not speak.

But when spring season comes,

The cuckoo, and crow speaks, and gets
identified.

The relationships are always good from a
distance,

When it is close, it does not have respect like
the water of pond.

The eyes are salty, and the lips are sweet like
honey,

And there is nothing wrong with it.

Because sweet tastes good after salty and,

Salty tastes good after sweet.

Similarly, the image of my sweetheart is settled
in my eyes.

Where can the second image fit?

The cuckoo remains silent during the rainy
season.

Because she knows that at this time the frogs
will speak,

No one will ask for her.

This is the downside of being very rich

Whenever the money decreases, he feels very
sad.

Therefore, it is better to be poor.

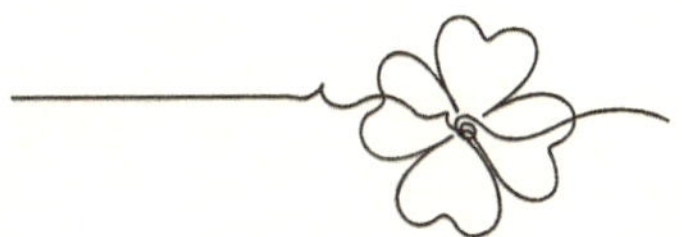

When there are bad days, one should sit
quietly.

And when the good days will come, all the
work will happen automatically.

Friendship with a man of mean mentality is
just like friendship with the dog.

It licks the mouth when it loves, and bites
when it is angry.

Its sure that after this birth, we will not meet
again.

Therefore, one should make friendship with
everyone,

And one should not have enmity with
anyone.

Think carefully, neither sword is of the iron nor
of the blacksmith,

But it belongs to the one who attack with it on
someone.

The God did to me what a bow does to an
arrow,

First it pulls towards itself then it throws away.

One should help someone as much as possible.

Because nothing remains in this world,

All what remains is to say.

There is happiness in every stage of human life.

One just needs to find it from his inner side.

There is joy in the deed and devotion also,

But above all, there is joy of peace.

Beyond pleasure of deed and devotion,

The complete pleasure of peace lies in the self-knowledge.

With what face will you go to the court of
God?

Because you never felt ashamed.

There is strong relationship between
resentment too,

The man lives both in the heart and mind.

My own people have taught me.

That no one is yours here.

I am helpless but I am not a labourer,

So, O'my life give me a little less trouble.

I spent my mornings selling in my office.

So that I can buy something in the evening
and take it to home.

I kept roaming around all my life in torn
cloths.

When I will die then I will be dressed in new
cloths.

Not being able to donate is a different matter,

But not donating despite being capable is
betrayal of trust.

Mind is such kind of land wherever the seed
of which mentality would be sown,

It would give the same result.

Every time of your life is fixed.

A very place of your life is fixed.

You do not go anywhere, but you are taken there.

You are not playing the game, but HE is playing the game.

She never gave a rose to that man,

But she did not give the man's share of love to
anyone else.

Sometimes our intention is only for friendship,

But sometimes love happens that we do not
even realise.

We are living under some strange intoxication,

Ever since we met you, we have been lost.

They will betray you by making you theirs.

What will they give the pages of the books of
the past?

If you would have burnt in the light and heat
of the sun,

then you would have reached your destination.

A man's heart it not bad, not every person is
cruel.

Winds are not always responsible for
extinguishing the lamp,

Sometimes, lamps got out due to lack of oil.

I think that for every examination,

someone has given him my home address.

If someone has a heart then there will be pain,

Perhaps there must be some story behind this.

After being separated from them it was as if
we died,

But his days also passed, and my days also
passed.

The day I will become wise, you will not be
able to understand me.

So, if I am crazy in your eyes then let me
remain mad.

When eyes saw the destination.

Why not seek feet advice now?

When the destination of the path of life is
death,

Then why not enjoy the journey now?

Why should not the moon be so proud?

When the nights have set him on his head.

The solution of your every problem is in your hands.

The man himself becomes thorn in the path of his happiness.

The world today cannot be changed, without changing the humans.

Your happiness, love, pains, troubles and joy are in your hands.

The joy of giving up own ego is something different.

Just surrender yourself to Gods will and infinite talent.

I was born with very soft heart,

But the experiences of the life turned me into
stone.

What is the era of pilgrimages?

Because we are far away from that for which
we desire.

Those people are very dangerous, who never
think, and never feel sad.

Caution is better than request, not every
handshaker is your friend.

The life is given more or less to everyone here,

But the death is given equally to everyone.

If you do not believe then wait,

But the morning has never broken its promise.

Do not measure the old friends with new
energy.

Do not break the bonds of relationships by
dishonesty.

The deities which were created by me with the
chisel of words.

Now they say not to sing songs,

those who used to praise my words.

There is amazing love in your eyes.

When I meet you, I get lost in your thoughts.

The one whom I love cannot be ordinary.

So, she is proud of herself, then there is no
surprise in this.

You are the only one whom I feel happy
seeing,

So do not be angry with me for God's sake.

At least you would have told me the reason for
not hearing me.

Were you angry with me or were thousands
with you like me.

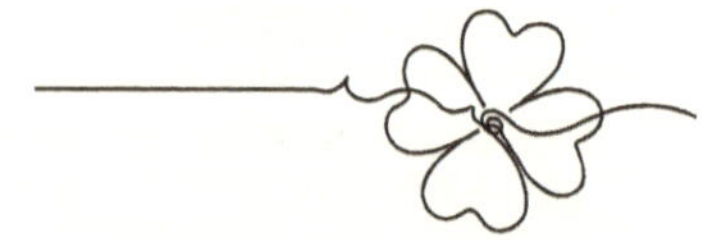

Life slips on the floor of the time.

I will tell you if I stay somewhere.

I am on a journey tell the death sometime.

What is bad if the lovers can read the eyes?

What is fun if something is said by the torque?

Many times, I tried to love someone else,

But apart from you, I could not find anyone
else.

Kunwar Bahadur Singh § 125

Everyone was smart at the time of committing crime.

But when the time of punishment came, everyone became innocent.

When your name was associated with name of someone else.

Although it was very small thing, but it touched my heart.

Well, everything gets repaired in the market,

but the wounds of the heart cannot be sowed.

Do not feel sad if they ignore you,

because hurting the heart of loved ones has become a tradition in the world.

I would have left this world long ago,

I would have died before coming into
existence.

I would have been scattered like pearls,

if I had not met you in life.

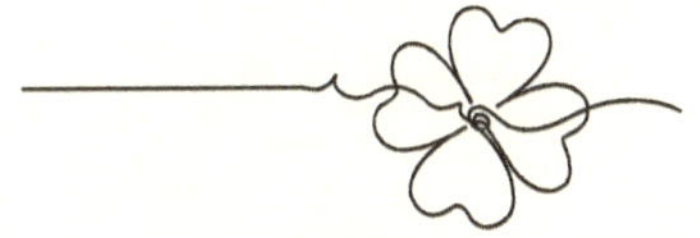

The emotions change in the path of the age.

The condition changes in the storm of the time.

I think I should break the record of working to perform the work,

But the idea changes to see the pay scale.

Nothing is kept in the lines of the hands,

Here crown fell with a few fists,

When that building was built, many houses
were built,

But the labour we who had fallen, and died
was only in the newspapers.

Kunwar Bahadur Singh § 129

The first wealth is wealth,

and the second wealth is health.

The third wealth is success,

and the fourth wealth is boldness.

The fifth wealth is friendliness,

and the sixth wealth is skilfulness.

The seventh wealth is dignity,

and the eighth wealth is memory.

That wealth is not precious,

which you have kept in your iron safe.

The real wealth is that,

Which we create inside us through discipline.

Friends do not get into trouble now by
mistake,

Because your own, and strangers will be
identified.

There is hatred which people understand with
in a moment,

But there is love which people spend their lives
trying to understand.

I fell while lifting someone from the ground,

Then it happened and someone trampled
upon me.

O' my God,

You only do wonders,

Seeing the destiny of the glass,

you handed over the stone to someone.

One who does not get angry, and does not
even talk,

How difficult is to convince that man?

Leave something incomplete in life,

Because it is not necessary for every journey to
have a destination.

Some remained in someone

And someone got swept away in others.

Everything was a game of one's own destiny.

It is his old habit to laugh at my situation.

So, if ever he is sad then tell him my story.

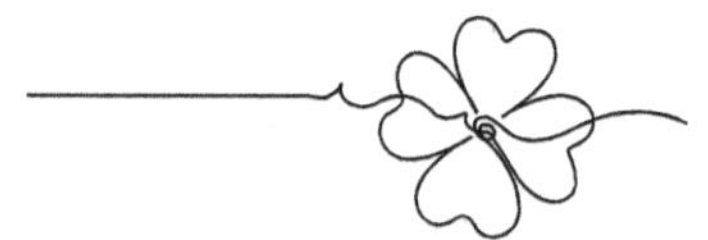

Whenever I asked permission to go,

She said yes with her tongue but said no with her eyes.

One day everything will be okay.

The whole life passed by listening to this.

When people start crying over small things,

Then understand that the person is very broken
from inside.

When someone will truly love you,

So, he will worry about you all the time.

Your one look bought me,

Otherwise, I was also very proud that no one
could buy me.

Who sees thousands of mistakes in me today,

Sometimes he used to say that you are mine as
you are.

The mother travels far to fill water every day.

She fills a pitcher of water and brings it on her
head every day,

She gets wet every day,

Thus, she celebrates the festival of
Holi every day.

The mirrors in my house have also become
unfaithful like you,

When I see my own face, it becomes your
face.

I am the one who could not understand myself
till date,

Who knows what some people think of me?

There should be some dreams in the eyes,

And some hopes in the heart,

Just breathing is not called life.

Everyone asks, how is the life going?

No one asks, how I am living my life.

If you will look in the pocket of a smiling man,

There you will find a wet handkerchief.

I was a traveller earlier,

and I am still a traveller today.

Earlier, I used to search my loved ones,

Now I search myself.

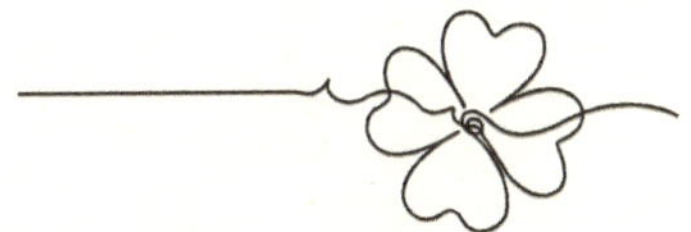

I loved her very badly, but she broke me.

I do not know who has written my fate?

He left everything of mine incomplete,

And everyone is sad here,

Someone is sad with in and someone sad from outside.

One pain did all the magic, now do I not feel any trouble.

Sir, please maintain your good manners in every condition.

The resentment has its own place, and salute has its own place.

Someone got his wish,

Someone was left with only his promise.

I have a habit of smiling,

So, even thousands of sorrows cannot change
my nature.

I have only stolen the heart of an innocent girl,

I have not stolen anyone's treasure.

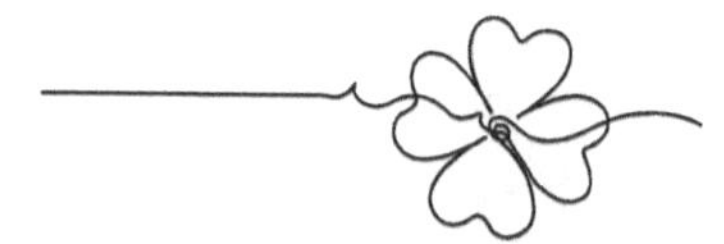

I know that I am a stranger myself,

You call me stranger thus you have a valid
point.

There was a lot of bitterness in his words,

That was his last letter not even the termites
ate it.

I have fight with all the Gods living on the
earth.

So, my God of the sky take care of my fate.

Everyone left me before reaching the
destination.

But my poverty turned out to be very much
loyal to me.

If you want to hate me then keep your resolve strong,

Otherwise, if there is even a little mistake, you will fall in love with me.

Still, he did not understand the depth of my words.

I said every word that means love.

Silences also speak to those who cannot talk.

Even people also love those people whom they
never met.

The intoxication of her memories
was very sweet.

The time passed and we got used to it.

I had a dream to touch the entire sky.

But I sold my wings to meet some of my
needs.

I have bought the tossing and turning by
selling my sleep.

I have become a merchant of my memories.

I wish this life of mine,

Would have been spent in not understanding.

Because my wisdom,

Took away a lot from me.

The world become intelligent,

By cheating others.

But I became criminal,

By trusting everyone.

I am sitting in the room with everything
scattered.

I had a dream somewhere now that too is lost.

There is both good and bad in me,

The seeker should think what does he wants.

If someone is angry with you then please win
quickly,

Because the separation often wins in the battle
of pride.

I had never remained alone by the grace of
God,

When you are not with me, then your
memories remain with me.

The doctor said this after holding my vein,

He is alive for whom you have died.

Do not come towards me after you become someone's.

Because separation in love is not justified.

The marks of your footsteps are present on my heart,

I will not anyone else pass after you.

My efforts always failed,

Sometimes, to get you, and sometimes to forget you.

This is the only thing I have written in my life.

I had very strong relationships with very weak people.

O 'my God for whom you have created heaven?

Who is not culprit here?

There used to be a lot of crowds in my
gathering,

But when I started telling truth everyone left.

This is not necessary to throw a stone to break
someone,

Changing the tone also breaks a lot.

Even prayers do not work,

When the person leaving decides to leave any
person.

People remain silent only in two conditions,

Is it either wisdom or any compulsion?

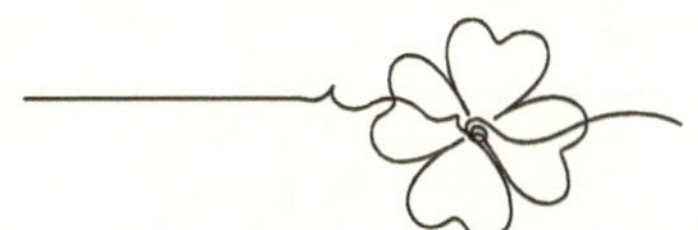

Kunwar Bahadur Singh § 157

I tried many relationships, but the results were
one,

Need is everything, love is nothing.

Sometimes meeting is good,

because I have seen the respect decreases due
to daily commuting.

The time does not have to be special,

But the time is essential to be special.

Whenever I see him through these eyes,

Whatever the day may be, it becomes my
festival.

I have loved you, I have not fallen in your
love,

Because of your presence or absence.

Those people who once used to say that we
never want to lose you.

They have forgotten me.

I am looking for that kind of love,

Which starts with hate and ends with love.

Sometimes when you do not have any one to
support you,

Then stand once in front of the mirror and
smile.

O' my lord,

Do not ask me for an account of my sins,

Because it was your pen who wrote my
destiny.

What does that man know about the value of
true love,

Who always loved the body.

The life is just this much of a thing,

I came to this world, stayed there, and left.

This is my only fault sir,

The decisions which were to be taken with our minds,

We took them with our heart.

As soon as you are beautiful,

Everyone will praise you,

But the one who praises you when your face
gets wrinkles, is your real lover.

There is no greater beauty than faith.

There is no fragrance better than character.

If you are unable to sleep even,

Please extinguish the lamp.

Because I do not like that someone burning all
night long.

You do not do what people want you to do.

So sometimes you become bad without doing
anything wrong.

You took away my life from me,

Now you have left me for nowhere.

The man who has the habit of speaking the
truth,

He cannot adjust himself anywhere.

When your own people will harass you,

Then you will remember me very much again.

The fun is when you keep laughing even after losing,

Is it not strange to always win?

What is wrong if I do my prayers myself.

I have heard from a saint that God resides with in myself.

When I see a smiling face,

Then I pray that he should not fall in love with anyone.

She was thinking a way to forget me,

I made all her problems easier by getting angry
with her.

When I saw her talking with others then I felt
very bad,

Then I remembered what relation do I have
with her?

Someone told me that you are a very nice man,

I also told him that this is the only my trouble.

Some people maintain relationships by melting like wax.

Some people burn relationships like fire.

Everyone gets time to change their life.

But you did not get life to change the time.

The world is full of selfishness, and no one is
special,

When I need someone, no one is there.

Why be afraid of death,

It lasts only for few moments,

Fear is from the life,

Which lasts for years.

Only some people can understand,

Not everyone can understand,

The story of heart and tears of the eyes.

Everything is mortal in this world,

After a time, everything gets destroyed.

After a certain time, this body would also be
destroyed.

Only the soul remains which keeps changing
from one shape to another.

Let your life flow into the permanence of
change.

Coming, and going is here like a changing
state,

So only change is permanent in the life.

We should accept it and move forward because
this is the truth of the life.

I will live openly latter on,

I kept explaining myself in the morning and evening.

But responsibilities kept coming, and the fun of the life kept on going.

Do not get discouraged like this after seeing the difficulties.

Seeing your courage, the destination will bow their heads.

I did not stop her, so she went away,

My helplessness kept looking her from the
distance.

Whatever I used to write with my tears on the
sand,

That story of mine remained incomplete.

One who wastes time, regrets it all his life,

Because the past time never comes back again
in the life of anyone.

We should not be happy in the sorrow of
anyone,

We should not be sorrowful in the happiness
of anyone.

Our love should remain intact.

Our happinesses should remain intact.

Our promises should remain intact.

Our obligations should remain intact.

Our gratitude should remain intact.

Our these impressions should remain intact.

Which is half, it does not mean that is
incomplete.

Which is enough, it does not mean that it is
complete.

Everywhere, the money is not needed to help
anyone,

Somewhere, the desires are needed to help
someone.

The teacher said to the pupil that the destiny is
more powerful than the deed,

The profit and loss, the life and death,

And the respect and disrespect are in the hands
of God.

O' my God do not give me the company of
the wicked men.

I would like to live in the hell than to live in
the company of wicked men.

Every leaf, and every bud knows my condition,

The flower knows or does not know, but the
garden knows very well.

I became, you became, and everyone became
slave of her curls.

This I know, you know, and everyone knows
very well.

Whatever happens inside, is visible outside.

Our actions express who we are.

External expressions are the indication of our internal state.

Therefore, first, we must become simple from inside.

Only then, we will be able to understand the values and the essence of human life.

Solution of all problems is only possible by being simple.

I have seen very blue sky.

I have seen green leaves.

I have seen very quiet winds.

I have seen very deep rivers.

I have seen very high mountains.

I have seen dense forests.

I have seen very bright rays.

I have seen very light clouds.

But I have often seen, the love in the core of
the heart very heavy.

I have seen very blue sky.

Kunwar Bahadur Singh § 181

O' Secrecy, I want to go inside you.

O' Knowledge, I want to go away from you.

O' Mystery, I want to see your mouth to drive
away the curls.

O' Experiences, free me up to the limit of
innocence, and motionlessness.

O' attraction, I always oppose you.

O' life, I want to come while walking inside
you.

I have no interest in proving myself,

I am what, the world has understood me to be.

Tears come out even if slightest mistake
happens.

Applying the soot to someone eyes is not a
game.

I am away from you for your happiness,

Do not think that I do not feel sad for you.

The mirror is spreading the evil of fraud among
the people.

Its telling to everyone that there is no one
beautiful as you.

It hurts a lot if the way of speaking becomes
stranger,

It does not matter if the faces become strangers.

Let me remain deserted like this,

Let me be upset, I do not like happiness.

Where there is no custom of separation,

I want to meet him in that world.

The one who gets the chance will drink my
blood.

There is strange sweetness in my poor blood.

We can just feel that whatever we are
thinking,

This means that we can change our emotions
by changing the thinking.

The moment we stop thinking, happiness
beings.

Overthinking is the root cause of all sufferings.

No matter, how ordinary a man is,

He is definitely special for someone.

If I spread my leg my head hits the wall,

O' My life you have given me less space than
a grave.

How much beautiful are you?

And how much heartbroken am I?

It is sad that we both will die one day too.

If you will know my problem, then you will
crave for my laughter too.

What was not possible, has become possible,

When I found the river, I lost my thirst,

I find peace in your words,

We do not long to talk to you just like that.

I do not want to love someone,

But there was pain in my destiny, so I fall in
love.

We come to you for two hours,

I did not intend to live with you for the rest of
life,

If you have gone away, please come back
sometime.

I am very sad in these days.

Do not torment me like this.

If you love me then make love with me with
my shortcomings,

Otherwise, I do not need your kindness.

Breathing is not the name of life,

Some people die even after living.

I have hidden so many sorrows in this way.

O' life, I have always spent you with
laughing.

Your memories one enough tried to come
again, and again.

My mind has understood that now I should
not remain restless.

The wound heals but the scar remains.

Memories never end with distances.

The thoughts continuously go on in our mind.

We can give right direction,

To our thoughts going on in our mind.

It's important for us to understand the idea correctly,

because this is self-realization.

Otherwise, we cannot find through,

This is the path of peace, and satisfaction.

Although, your hands are not in my hands,

Even then there should be a hope.

This holy feeling should always remain in our hearts that,

We will definitely meet with each other one day at any time.

He was used to darkness, so he became the
moon.

The sky became angry from the day, I called
you moon.

Why do not we consider ourselves as kings,

Because I am also seeing the same sun and
moon, which they have seen.

It is very easy to love someone,

And it's foolish to hate someone.

If we want to live together then,

We will have to learn tolerance.

This is necessary for the survival of the human
civilisation on this land.

We must learn to live together instead of only
seeking God.

Every money is not the money,

There is a difference between the money,

Earned by honesty and dishonesty.

The money earn by dishonesty is just like
poison,

Which cannot be digested by any person.

If you include someone else in your disrespect,

Then you will be able to save your half respect.

After a certain age,

A man ceased to be a man, and he becomes a story.

Those who escape from life,

They are killed by the age gradually.

They are happy who are busy in their works.

He is sorrowful,

Who does not want to see the happinesses of others.

It is not necessary to run always to get something.

So many things such as,

Peace, happiness, and satisfaction can be obtained by staying together.

Give us a day off from your memories,

There should be Sunday in love section too.

Love is love, it should be expressed,

You must be sick of your face too.

We are just interested in a false assurance,

Who says promise love to you.

I know what my status in this city is.

I am so proud because of you.

Who knows the meaninglessness of the life,

One who crosses while laughing the
river of life.

And this means meaningless hero,

Lives happily in every condition.

We should not try to find out the meaning of
the life,

But we should try to enjoy the life in every
condition.

Man is moving forward with the help of
knowledge.

There is no shadow of sorrow left in his life.

There is no more fear of ghosts, and animals,

But the fear of the man for the man remains.

There are no visible signs of getting rid of these
fears,

So, the strength, and kindness are necessary for
the fearlessness.

Although I was not living in your world,

But I was living in you somewhere.

The moon, and stars were in your curls,

and I was living like clouds there.

I made you sky, and was living on the earth,

I used to live in your these, deserted eyes for a
long time.

The day is like dark night in my own eyes.

The shadow was with me,

And the shadow is with me.

Only her memories remained in the house of
my heart,

I was left alone,

And she has gone away to break my heart.

The flowers got separated from the branches,

And all the leaves fell from the tree.

I do not know,

Why his own separated from him,

May be that is why God also lives completely alone.

Wherever the lamp will go,

There will be the light.

Because the lamp does not have his own
house.

You must always listen to your friends,

Because nobody listens to them in their own
house.

I will take some time to search myself,

So, if you come back then tell me sometime
before.

The lips have this complain to the eyes that
they speak truth,

They speak better, and they also speak more.

My eyesight which is not sorrowful to see
your sorrows,

This does not mean that I do not love you.

O' my dear, your picture is present in my heart,

I cannot wait for any other one except you.

By mistake, I stepped in your city,

This little step betrayed me.

Do not make my destination too far away,

I have taken a little step in your love.

What did I ask from you and what did you
give me?

You started giving air to the fire of my heart.

The difficulties of the path also started to give
me way,

To see my courage, zeal, and sentiment.

You cheater, you have openly cheated me,

Thus, my friend has openly given me a
message of deception.

Its okay that you have openly cheated me,

But I was also blamed for the loneliness not
without reason,

I have billed your poison by becoming nectar.

But you have offered me again the cup of the
poison,

When will you give me rest in my life,

You kept on deceiving me by being my
companion.

You have reaped, what you have sown,

You still think that you must not lose more.

This is the beginning of your destructions,

You must be ruined even more.

The one who blesses,

Should keep on blessing,

The king of this territory is less able to hear.

He is begging from the God for himself,

He does not know that HE gives only true to
man's nature.

How our last time will be,

It will not be decided by the money with us.

It will be decided by,

Our good and bad deeds done by us.

We will have to appease him if he is angry,
We will have to show our love.
We will have to laugh to hide our wound,
We are forbidden to talk to anyone.

Always accept praise with humility,

And always take criticism seriously.

Someone has rightly said,

Find out short comings in my character
without any hindrance,

Because if you are not there,

Then who will correct me truly?

A crow can suppress the voice of cuckoo,

But a crow cannot make his voice melodious
like cuckoo.

Similarly, a wicked man can defame a famous
man,

But he cannot become famous like famous
man.

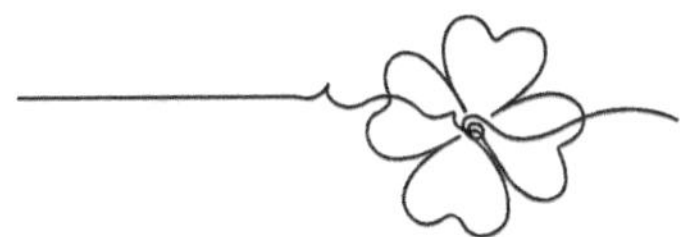

Whatever he wanted to say, he said,

But his head was bleeding badly.

He was released from the prison,

But the entire sky was disturbed extremely.

Look the examination paper was snatched
from you,

Now your examination is over.

Who placed a rose on his grave,

Who became his lover?

Just by saying one thing of yours.

The whole world became speechless.

The doomsday strikes.

Somewhere in the world every day.

Thus, the sun becomes cup of blood,

Somewhere or the other every day.

Where can I find the words to praise him?

Who brings the sun out of the darkness every
day.

You see, what a beautiful view it is,

You see the scene through my eyes once.

The moon has come to meet you only,

You go and see on your terrace at least once.

Your happiness will become double,

You try laughing with me once.

This world is always a test,

You should take part in this examination and
see once.

You will get the right to live in this world,

You should try dying for your rights once.

Ego is the biggest illusion of our life,

Which does not allow us to see life to its
fullest.

We get this illusion that we are also
something,

But what are we, we do not know at the least?

The day we will understand that the ego is the
biggest liar of life,

That very day life will become oriented
towards peace and pleasure.

Kunwar Bahadur Singh § 217

The sky is always awake,

Except sky who will make the moon alert?

There is no count of the wounds on my heart.

After shedding all his blood,

Who will populate this desert?

Now who will take the loan from death?

When, I have spent my whole life in debt.

Who will believe you at this moment?

Who will wait for the morning at this
moment?

The giving up is your biggest crime,

The best way to succeed is to try one more
time.

You must start where you are,

You should use whatever you have.

You do whatever you can do,

Comfortably for your advancement.

You always remember it that if there is no
conflict,

There will be no development.

O' my sins, calm down,

Do not cry too much for the welfare of the
world.

Because this time is bathed in the nectar,

This is not the right time, and place for tears.

Today the festival of spring is being celebrated
here,

Therefore, keep your sorrows within your
heart,

Because the mango flowers and the grooms
crown,

Do not faint on seeing tears.

What is the point of crying,

If it does not melt the stones?

What is it the use of shedding tears,

If it does not break the heart into pieces?

What is the use of drinking wine,

If it does not make a man to forget the world
after drinking?

What is the use of that youth,

Which is afraid of dying?

We do not need to fear,

If the difficulties come in our life.

The life is very beautiful,

And we should have the confidence.

Whenever, the bad times come before us,

We should stand like a mountain.

The life is a beautiful cloth made by,

Threads of pleasure, and pain.

I will embrace,

All the flames of fire one by one.

I will endure severe suffering,

And I will enjoy unlimited pleasure.

There should be nothing left worth knowing,

if I have come in this world then,

I must do this much at least.

Let the life go bigger and bigger,

As I get closer to it.

Kunwar Bahadur Singh § 223

I have not been able to understand this
mystery till now,

Why do the cluster of the stars shine so much
in the sky?

The thirst of my eyes, is not quenched,

Although I stand and keep watching towards
the sky.

I am a lover, and you are the ocean of
knowledge,

This is the only difference between you and
me.

The heart which sees with love,

That can never be understood through logic
and intelligence

Getting happiness in married life,

Completely depends on fortune not on the efforts,

Ask to the lamp, and not to the moon,

How much starry the night was?

The night in my mind became bright,

Seeing your rainbow-like image.

The bonds of life became lose, and the
consciousness,

Merged into the ocean of your lovely
appearance.

When you looked at me with your heart,

Filled with love and loving eyes.

Then my dew drops had become colourful,

And tears of joy started falling from my eyes.

The man burns on this side,

And the tobacco burns on that side.

There is ash on both the sides every day.

I came to this side of hopes, and desires,

Because a wise man emerged inside me today.

We kept you looking into every flower, and

You kept on flying in the breeziness.

We closed our eyes for a while,

And you started laughing among the stars.

When I opened my eyes after crying,

I saw someone just like you in my tears.

But when I tried to touch you,

Then you rolled away and hid in the fog,

Leaving me alone among the sufferers.

The God has given us eyes to see the world.

The God has given us a nose to smell the
things of the world.

The God has given us mouth to pray the God.

The God has given us ears to listen the stories
of God.

The God has given us hands to give charity to
poor people.

The God has given us feet to go on the
pilgrimage.

The God has given us everything best,

But the God has given us stomach to lose our
respect.

Kunwar Bahadur Singh § 229

The world talks about me because of you,

The world talks about you because of me.

If you raise your hands against atrocities on
me,

then I will say that you love me.

O' my God, give me livelihood with respect.

I will never complain you about less those are
abundant.

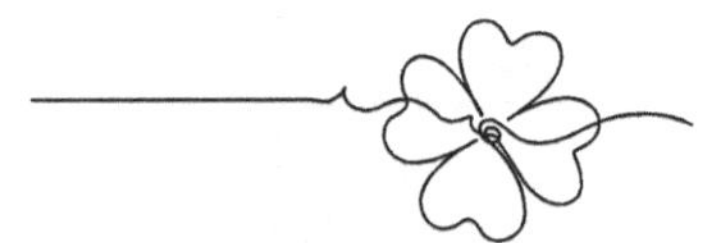

You are the best, and my luck is better than yours,

Because of which I got the opportunity to see your face.

How can a man find happiness from wealth?

What makes me happiest is the honest people around me.

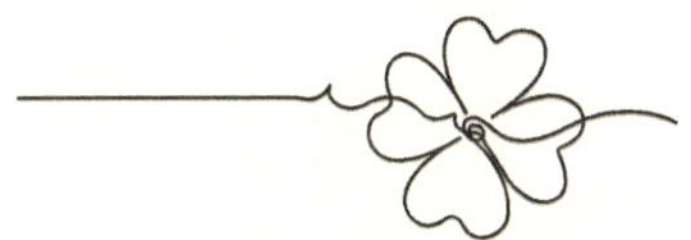

O'my omnipotent, omnipresent, and omniscient,

How do I change my habit of waiting for you?

Now this is beyond control of my heart, and intellect.

Although I have not seen you,

but still, I remember you.

As there is such a fragrance of your love in my heart.

No matter, how clear the water is, it is not a mirror.

Not every stone is God among the stones.

It takes lifetime to reach destination,

No one becomes great by raising his heels.

Those who do not recognise the knowledge,
and virtue,

Such people remain engaged in useless things.

Such people stay away from the real Goal,

And keep chasing the useless things.

A man should be courageous,

And he needs to look into himself.

If we look inside himself then he will realise
that,

the gold and silver are not outside, but within
himself.

Your separation from me was an excuse,

And I had to bear this loss in the love.

Anybody may give you place in heart,

But there was only one place for me.

When the time changes, the winds also
change.

But at least you should not have left me.

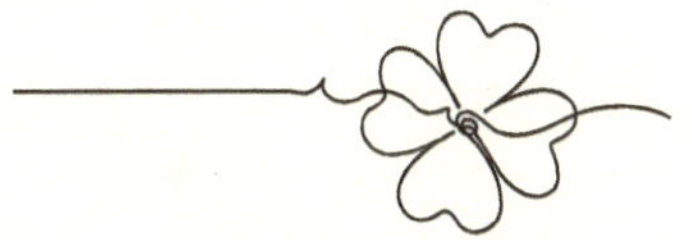

It's not my habit to live in loneliness,

Although now a days, I am not physically fit.

O' Madam, these are the paths of the love,

Wherever is the entrance, but there is no exit.

I do not like butterflies,

Sitting on the body of the flowers.

I do not like thunder bolts,

Falling from your eyes.

From the day she came in my lane, believe me,

Since that day, I do not like to sit inside the house.

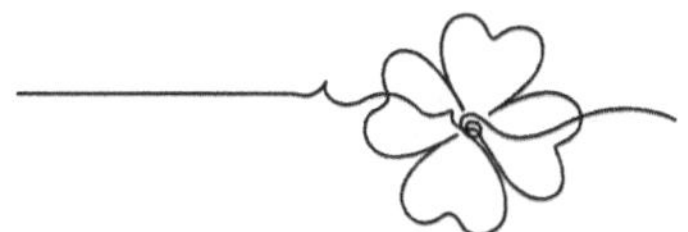

The stone always lives among the stones,

And this is not without reason,

The clean water might not become the mirror
in any condition.

No one can become big by raising his heels,

The whole life of the man expires in achieving
the destination.

The favour of the friends should not be kept
unpaid,

The salt should not be kept near the wound.

The flower should be kept in the apiary,

The watchman should not be kept for the
beauty.

The tears should come in the eyes,

Either on the pretext of sorrow or smile.

The eyes should not be kept dry for the long
time.

I also know, how to look fully in the faces.

I also know how to interchange the glances.

I will accept everything by going near to anyone.

I also know how to embrace anyone.

I touched the snake by relying on the sandal
wood,

But the snake did not spit out the poison

O' my leader the public gathered by relying on
your oration.

Now you should blossom buds as per your
commitments,

The butterflies came by relying on spring
season.

Because they sow the seeds by relying on the
rainy season.

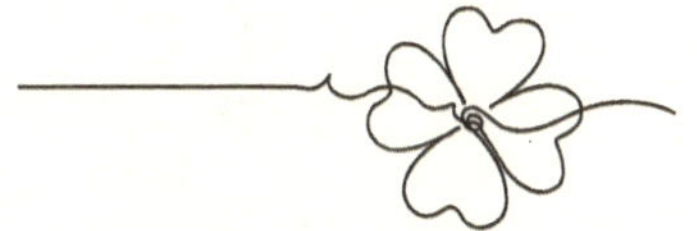

Kunwar Bahadur Singh § 241

Today we are the body,

Tomorrow, we will be remembered only.

I have moved on long ago towards desire,

Tell the time to come with me.

This is true that today is not in my hands.

But a little of that will remain in my poems.

I have distributed the tiredness,

Between the body and mind,

But I could not distribute,

The sentiment of love between the heart and
mind.

He exclaimed to listen that he could not get
success,

The shadow came near the shadow and asked
for the shade.

The tree asked to another tree,

Why are you weeping?

The tree said, O' my brother,

Our own's are cutting me with the help of an
wooden axe.

We should not fear from the difficulties of the
path,

When we have decided to go ahead with the
power of determination.

This life is the game of chess at every moment,

So, we should not fear from the tricks of the
deception.

Your shadow is in my heart, and
Your memories are in my eyes.
How can I forget you,
Because your love is in my breaths.

I am the Sun,

So do not fear from the darkness,

This country is mine,

And I am not living here on tenancy.

This is not the time,

To alienate yourself.

This is the time,

To come forward and protect the country.

The branches of the tree,

May fight against any branch of the tree,

There might be any desire,

But she may fight against any desire.

You do not know about the nature of the
women of my nation.

She can fight with the lord of death for her
vermilion.

I just did not trust him,

As he was devoted to his family in real sense.

When I became father,

Then I realized that how much love was in his voice.

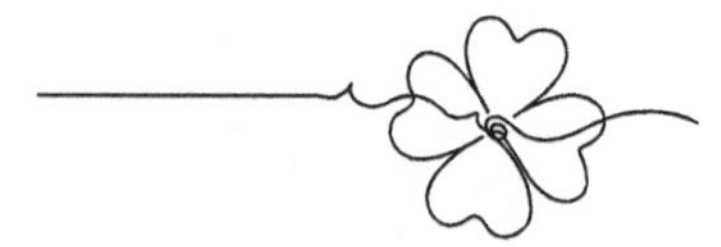

You should give a twist to the story.

If I am bad, then leave me in solitary.

Your silence is harassing me at every moment,

Now you should burst the blisters of your
heart.

You are very much anxious to break
something,

I am presenting my heart to you.

You may break it at any moment.

Kunwar Bahadur Singh § 249

How will the tree grow in the deserted land,
and

How will the interest come in an uninteresting
story?

How will you see the difference between the
good, and bad,

When your only objective is to earn money?

The man who will always be sorrowful to his
neighbours,

How will he get peace through his prayers?

O' my friend, I cannot pay the price of
friendship,

O' my friend, forgive me, I cannot bow down
my head.

I am not mat dust, I am a living man,

You cannot blow me to put it on your hand.

I tore your arrogance into pieces,

You thought that you can beat me with in
second.

Although I keep my feet on the earth,

But I do believe in the supremacy.

Although, I do not have a beautiful face,

But I have a beautiful heart in my body.

You may search your fate in the lines of your
palm,

But I have faith in the mercy of the Almighty.

Perhaps, one day my turn will also come,

When they will see that we are merged in
their heart.

When our praises will adorn their lips,

And we will climb up on the height of
achievement.

The defeat happens when it is accepted,

And victory comes when there is
determination.

Whose glimpse makes you desirous,

She can be recognized even in the curtain,

There is not always gain in the trade of love,

Sometimes there might be loss also in this
trade.

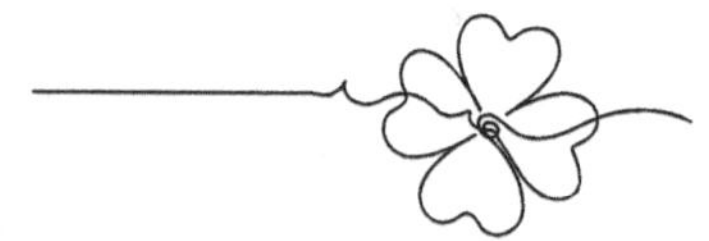

Somewhere the lamp should be burnt in the
temples,

Some where the prayers should be performed
in the mosques.

There are so many Gods in my city,

But I do not know about the humanity.

Even if we are separated, we remain hand in
hand,

Let it be a matter of something like this.

I am sleeping to see your dreams,

May God let your night remain in my eyes.

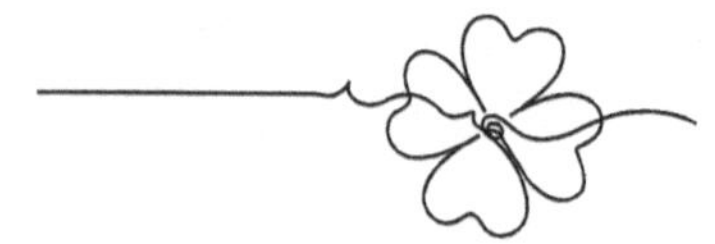

Nobody will bring the moon for you,

So, keep shining always your face.

You should also get some work from your lips,

So, keep smiling while talking with everyone.

The light and heat of the sun goes to become
sorrowful,

So, come to dry the clothes on the terrace.

Who says to you to join the hearts.

At least shake hands to show it to the others.

I have fallen in love of a lovely moon light,

I think, how do I express my thought?

Let the world keep looking at you.

I think, how to arrest you in my heart?

I have fallen in love of a beautiful women.

I think, how do I express my thought?

I gaze on the roof, but you do not come on the
roof,

I am helpless and troubled,

How can I see you O' my moonlight?

We will have to be more cautious,
Because this world is very much crooked.
It desires only beautiful faces,
That's why we will have to be well dressed.

Although you always do many favours,

Even then my complications do not
disentangle.

Do not take my words as false,

She loves me more than her life.